This fun **Phonics** reader

belongs to

_____

Ladybird Reading
Phonics
BOOK 3

Contents

A catalogue record for this book is available from the British Library

Published by Ladybird Books Ltd
80 Strand London WC2R 0RL
A Penguin Company

4 6 8 10 9 7 5 3
© LADYBIRD BOOKS LTD MMVI
LADYBIRD and the device of a Ladybird are trademarks of Ladybird Books Ltd

ISBN-13: 978-1-84646-327-3
ISBN-10: 1-84646-327-0

Printed in Italy

Hot Fox

by Dick Crossley
illustrated by Sue King

introducing the short **o** sound,
as in hot

Fox went box, box, box.

He went hop, hop, hop.

Fox went jog, jog, jog, up to the top.

Are you too hot, Fox?

nod nod nod

Tom's Dog

by Mandy Ross

illustrated by Rosalind Beardshaw

more on the short <u>o</u> sound,
as in dog

Tom's dog has
lots of spots.

Tom and Bob do
not have spots.

splot!

Now Tom and Bob have
lots of spots.

And Tom's dog has
not got spots.

Snug as a Bug

by Mandy Ross
illustrated by Marjolein Pottie

introducing the short **u** sound,
as in bug

Here is a bug and

here is a rug.

Here is a bug in a rug.

Here is a bug who is snug in a rug. Goodnight!

Yum Yum!

by **Dick Crossley**
illustrated by **Karl Richardson**

more on the short **u** sound,
as in mud

Take a mug of bugs

a jug of slugs,

and a cup of mud.

Put it all in a tub
and mush it up.

Yum! Yum!

Lunch is fun!

The Tip Top Chip Shop

by Richard Dungworth
illustrated by Sami Sweeten

introducing the **ch** , **sh**
and **th** sounds

This is the Tip Top
Fish and Chip Shop.

This is the man who
chops the chips…

at the Tip Top
Fish and Chip Shop.

Thin chips, thick chips,
lick your lips chips.

I like chips.

I wish I had a big dish of fish and chips.

I want thin chips, thick chips, lick your lips chips.

So I will dash with my
cash to the Fish and
Chip Shop.

For my thin chips, thick chips, lick your lips chips.

HOW TO USE
Phonics
BOOK 3

The stories in Book 3 introduce your child to two of the five short vowel sounds – o as in fox and u as in mud – and the ch, sh and th sounds. They will help your child begin reading simple words containing these sounds.

- Read each story through to your child first. Familiarity helps children to identify some of the words and phrases.

- Have fun talking about the sounds and pictures together. What repeated sound can your child hear in each story?

- Help your child break new words into separate sounds (eg. h-o-t) and blend them together to say the word.

- Point out how words with the same written ending sound the same. If b-ug says 'bug', what does m-ug or r-ug say?

- Some common words, such as 'your', 'who' and even 'the', can't be read by sounding out. Help your child practise recognising words like these.

Phonic fun

Write down some of the simple story words on cards. Cut off the first letter (or the 'ch' 'sh' or 'th' beginning) from each. Help your child pair up beginnings with endings to make and read as many real or nonsense words as she can. Then cut the endings into separate letters, and play the game again.

Ladybird Reading
Phonics

Phonics is part of the Ladybird Reading range. It can be used alongside any other reading programme, and is an ideal way to practise the reading work that your child is doing, or about to do in school.

Ladybird has been a leading publisher of reading programmes for the last fifty years. **Phonics** combines this experience with the latest research to provide a rapid route to reading success.

The fresh quirky stories in Ladybird's twelve **Phonics** storybooks are designed to help your child have fun learning the relationship between letters, or groups of letters, and the sounds they represent.

This is an important step towards independent reading – it will enable your child to tackle new words by sounding out and blending their separate parts.

How Phonics works

- The stories and rhymes introduce the most common spellings of over 40 key sounds, known as phonemes, in a step-by-step way.

- Rhyme and alliteration (the repetition of an initial sound) help to emphasise new sounds.

- Bright amusing illustrations provide helpful picture clues and extra appeal.